PIONEER VALLEY EDUC

THE
MOON

SEAN FINNIGAN

TABLE OF CONTENTS

Have you looked at the moon? Did you ever wonder how far away it is? The moon is Earth's closest neighbor in space. It is 238,855 miles from Earth.

The moon is very different from Earth. There is no air on the moon. There are also no plants or animals living on the moon.

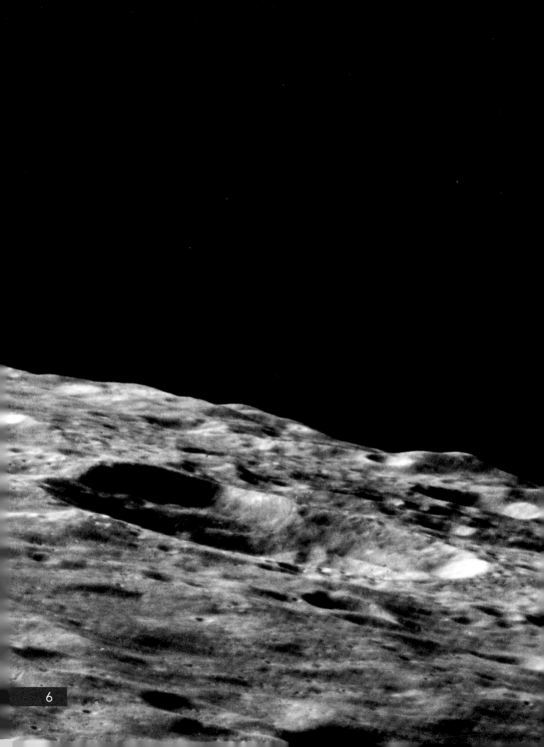

The moon has many holes, called **craters**.

Some of the craters are small.

Some are very big.

Scientists think the craters were made when rocks from space hit the moon.

The moon is always moving. The moon **orbits** around the Earth. It takes about 28 days for the moon to orbit Earth.

The moon also **rotates.**
It takes the moon
about 28 days
to rotate one time.

The moon sometimes

looks bright

in the night sky.

But the moon

does not make this light.

The moon **reflects** light

from the sun.

Sometimes it looks
like the moon
is changing shape.
This is because
we can only see
the part of the moon
that is reflecting light
from the sun.

As the moon orbits the Earth,
the sun's light shines
on different parts
of the moon.

➤ The shape of the lit part of the moon is called a
phase. The moon has eight phases.

first quarter

waxing
gibbous

waxing
crescent

full

new

waning
gibbous

waning
crescent

third
quarter

To learn more about the moon, scientists began to send spacecraft into space. The spacecraft went around the moon and took photographs.

On July 20, 1969,
an **astronaut**, Neil Armstrong,
was the first person
to walk on the moon.